Tell Me Why

WHY?

I Get Sunburned

Katie Marsico

Published in the United States of America by Cherry Lake Publishing
Ann Arbor, Michigan
www.cherrylakepublishing.com

Content Adviser: Lisa K. Militello, PhD, MPH, CPNP, The Ohio State University
Reading Adviser: Marla Conn, ReadAbility, Inc.

Photo Credits: © bonzodog/Shutterstock Images, cover, 1, 17; © Samuel Borges Photography/
Shutterstock Images, cover, 1, 9; © rmnoa357/Shutterstock Images, cover, 1, 11; © Lapina/Shutterstock
Images, cover, 1; © Gelpi JM/Shutterstock Images, cover, 1, 9; © NinaMalyna/Shutterstock Images, cover, 1;
© shalamov/Thinkstock, 5; © Suzanne Tucker/Shutterstock Images, 7; © Yu Lan/Shutterstock Images, 9;
© ttueni/Shutterstock Images, 13: © atikinka/Shutterstock Images, 17; © Fuse/Thinkstock, 19;
© Daniel M. Nagy/Shutterstock Images, 21

Library of Congress Cataloging-in-Publication Data

Marsico, Katie, 1980-
 I get sunburned / by Katie Marsico.
    pages cm. -- (Tell me why)
"Young children are naturally curious about themselves. Tell Me Why I Get Sunburned offers answers
to their most compelling questions about summer skin conditions. Age-appropriate explanations and
appealing photos encourage readers to continue their quest for knowledge. Additional text features and
search tools, including a glossary and an index, help students locate information and learn new words."
—Provided by publisher.
 Audience: 6-10.
 Audience: K to Grade 3.
 Includes bibliographical references and index.
 ISBN 978-1-63188-995-0 (hardcover) -- ISBN 978-1-63362-073-5 (pdf) -- ISBN
978-1-63362-034-6 (pbk.) -- ISBN 978-1-63362-112-1 (ebook) 1.
Sunburn--Juvenile literature. I. Title.

RL248.M37 2015
616.5'15--dc23

2014031828

Cherry Lake Publishing would like to acknowledge the work of The Partnership for 21st Century Skills.
Please visit www.p21.org for more information.

Printed in the United States of America
Corporate Graphics

Table of Contents

Looking Like a Lobster

Has Lina turned into a lobster? After spending all day at the beach, her skin is bright red! It also feels a little sore and warm.

Grandma looks closely at Lina's arms, neck, back, and face. She assures Lina that she is not turning into a sea creature. Instead, her rosy appearance is a sign that she got sunburned.

Too much time in the sun can result in sunburned skin.

Sunburn is the body's response when skin is **exposed** to too much sun. Grandma says that the sun gives off rays, or beams, of light.

People are able to view some of these rays but not all of them. For example, they don't see **ultraviolet (UV) light**. But just because UV rays are invisible doesn't mean they're not powerful!

Wearing clothing at the beach can help you protect your skin.

UV light is strong enough to damage skin **cells**. Too much exposure to UV rays often leads to sunburn. In some cases, it causes eye problems and skin **cancer**, too.

MAKE A GUESS!

Scientists have figured out that UV rays cause a person's skin to wrinkle faster. Are you able to guess why?

Wear waterproof sunscreen while swimming.

The Reason for Redness

Lina looks at herself in the mirror. Thanks to Grandma, she understands *why* she got sunburned. Yet she's still curious *how* it made her turn so red.

Grandma says that Lina's coloring is proof that her body is trying to heal itself. The **immune system** reacts to sunburn by causing more blood to flow toward the skin. Cells in the blood help repair damage created by UV rays.

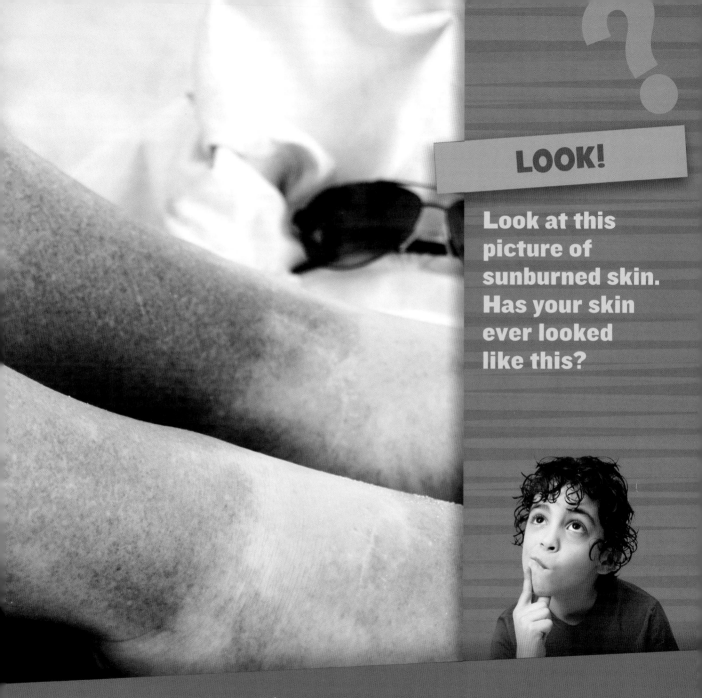

Look at this picture of sunburned skin. Has your skin ever looked like this?

Sunburned skin can be painful.

The body also responds to sunburn by producing more of a skin **pigment** called **melanin**. This pigment offers protection against UV rays. Increases in melanin production and blood flow are what make a person's skin swell and turn red.

If you do get sunburned, the redness should fade
in about a week.

How to Heal

Grandma warns Lina to be prepared for peeling as her skin heals.

Skin peels, or flakes off, as the body rids itself of damaged cells. Grandma explains that peeling is an important process. When damaged cells are allowed to build up, they sometimes lead to serious health problems such as cancer.

After a sunburn, skin often peels.

Meanwhile, Grandma mentions that there are many ways to deal with the soreness of being sunburned. Taking a cool bath is one. Another is treating the skin with lotions and **aloe vera**.

Grandma recommends staying out of the sun for a while. She also tells Lina not to scratch or pick the peeling skin, since this can sometimes lead to **infection**. Finally, Grandma says to keep **hydrated** by drinking plenty of water.

ASK QUESTIONS!

Why is it important to stay hydrated if you're sunburned? Ask a dermatologist! (That's a doctor who treats skin problems.)

Drinking water can help you stay hydrated.

Stay Safe in the Sun!

Now that she knows more about sunburns, Lina is already starting to feel a bit better. Still, she'd rather avoid them altogether. Grandma says that one solution is to use a strong, waterproof sunscreen. Wearing a hat and a cover-up helps, too. So does setting up a beach umbrella or tent.

Sunscreen helps protect your skin from burning.

Staying safe in the sun is also about timing. Grandma explains that UV rays are usually strongest between 10 a.m. and 4 p.m. So, it's best to either remain inside during that time or take regular breaks to go indoors.

Lina plans to put all of Grandma's tips into action when she returns to the beach. For the moment, however, she's ready for a cool bath, a little aloe, and a whole lot of shade!

Spending some time in a shaded spot can help you avoid getting sunburned.

Think About It

Have you ever noticed that lighter-skinned people seem to sunburn more easily than darker-skinned people? Why do you think this is?

The closer you are to the equator, the stronger the UV rays get. Find the equator on a globe. Then find Toronto and Miami. In which city do you think the UV rays would be more powerful?

The next time you visit the store, study all the different bottles of sunscreen. You probably see them labeled with numbers ranging from 2 to 100. What do you think these numbers mean?

Glossary

aloe vera (A-low VER-uh) a thick liquid produced by aloe plants that is often used in medicines and skin creams

cancer (KAN-suhr) a serious disease caused by abnormal cells that spread throughout the body

cells (SELZ) the smallest units that make up living things

exposed (ik-SPOHZD) open to contact with or unprotected from

hydrated (HYE-drayt-uhd) having the amount of fluid the body needs to work properly

immune system (ih-MYOON SIS-tuhm) the network of cells, tissues, and organs that work together to protect the body

infection (in-FEK-shuhn) an attack on the body by bacteria or viruses that are not normally present

melanin (MEH-leh-nen) a pigment that offers protection against the sun's ultraviolet light

pigment (PIG-muhnt) a natural substance that gives color to plants and animals

ultraviolet light (uhl-truh-VYE-luht LYTE) rays of light that are invisible to the human eye

Find Out More

Books:

Kennedy, Kimberling Galeti. *Hey, Don't Forget the Sunscreen!* Mustang, OK: Tate Publishing and Enterprises, LLC, 2013.

McAuliffe, Bill. *Cancer.* Mankato, MN: Creative Education, 2012.

Roca, Nuria, and Carol Isern. *The Sun.* Hauppauge, NY: Barrons Educational Series, Inc., 2014.

Web Sites:

Environmental Protection Agency (EPA)—SunWise Kids
www.epa.gov/sunwise1/kids/index.html
Learn additional facts about sun safety and test your knowledge with an online trivia quiz.

KidsHealth—How to Be Safe When You're in the Sun
http://kidshealth.org/kid/watch/out/summer_safety.html
Find out more about the best ways to avoid getting sunburned.

Index

About the Author

Katie Marsico is the author of more than 150 children's books. She lives in a suburb of Chicago, Illinois, with her husband and children.